Jazz Play-Along®

Book & Audio for B♭, E♭, C and Bass Clef Instruments

volume 155

PLAYBACK+
Speed • Pitch • Balance • Loop

Arranged and Produced by Mark Taylor and Jim Roberts

Arranged and Produced by Mark Taylor

	C Treble Instruments	B♭ Instruments	E♭ Instruments	C Bass Instruments
BLACK FROST	4	22	38	56
CHAIN REACTION	5	23	39	57
CHICAGO SONG	6	24	40	58
MAPUTO	20	21	54	55
RISE	8	26	42	60
SHAKER SONG	10	28	44	62
SILHOUETTE	12	30	46	64
TOURIST IN PARADISE	14	32	48	66
TURN YOUR LOVE AROUND	16	34	50	68
YOU MAKE ME SMILE	18	36	52	70

To access audio, visit:
www.halleonard.com/mylibrary

Enter Code
4212-9094-2851-1589

ISBN 978-1-61774-173-9

Visit Hal Leonard Online at
www.halleonard.com

World headquarters, contact:
Hal Leonard
7777 West Bluemound Road
Milwaukee, WI 53213
Email: info@halleonard.com

In Europe, contact:
Hal Leonard Europe Limited
1 Red Place
London, W1K 6PL
Email: info@halleonardeurope.com

In Australia, contact:
Hal Leonard Australia Pty. Ltd.
4 Lentara Court
Cheltenham, Victoria, 3192 Australia
Email: info@halleonard.com.au

Smooth Jazz Classics

Volume 155
Arranged and Produced by
Mark Taylor and Jim Roberts

Featured Players:

Graham Breedlove–Trumpet
John Desalme–Saxes
Tony Nalker–Piano
Jim Roberts–Bass
Todd Harrison–Drums
Manny Fishman–Shaker

**Recorded at Bias Studios, Springfield, Virginia
Bob Dawson, Engineer**

Each song has two tracks:

1) Split Track/Demonstration

Woodwind, Brass, Keyboard, and Mallet Players can use this track as a learning tool for melody style and inflection.

Bass Players can learn and perform with this track – remove the recorded bass track by turning down the volume on the LEFT channel.

Keyboard and **Guitar Players** can learn and perform with this track – remove the recorded piano part by turning down the volume on the RIGHT channel.

2) Backing Track

Soloists or **groups** can learn and perform with this accompaniment track with the RHYTHM SECTION only.

Black Frost

BY GROVER WASHINGTON, JR.
AND BOB JAMES

C VERSION

CHAIN REACTION

WORDS AND MUSIC BY
JOE SAMPLE

C VERSION

CHICAGO SONG

BY MARCUS MILLER

C VERSION

RISE

BY RANDY BADAZZ
AND ANDY ARMER

C VERSION

SHAKER SONG

BY JAY BECKENSTEIN

C VERSION

SILHOUETTE

BY KENNY G

C VERSION

TOURIST IN PARADISE

BY RUSS FREEMAN

C VERSION

Turn Your Love Around

WORDS AND MUSIC BY JAY GRAYDON,
STEVE LUKATHER AND BILL CHAMPLIN

C Version

YOU MAKE ME SMILE

BY DAVE KOZ AND JEFF KOZ

C VERSION

MAPUTO

BY MARCUS MILLER

MAPUTO

BY MARCUS MILLER

BLACK FROST

BY GROVER WASHINGTON, JR.
AND BOB JAMES

Bb VERSION

CHAIN REACTION

WORDS AND MUSIC BY
JOE SAMPLE

CHICAGO SONG

BY MARCUS MILLER

Bb VERSION

RISE

BY RANDY BADAZZ
AND ANDY ARMER

Bb Version

SHAKER SONG

BY JAY BECKENSTEIN

Bb VERSION

Silhouette

BY KENNY G

Bb VERSION

TOURIST IN PARADISE

BY RUSS FREEMAN

Bb VERSION

Turn Your Love Around

WORDS AND MUSIC BY JAY GRAYDON,
STEVE LUKATHER AND BILL CHAMPLIN

Bb VERSION

You Make Me Smile

BY DAVE KOZ AND JEFF KOZ

Bb VERSION

Black Frost

BY GROVER WASHINGTON, JR.
AND BOB JAMES

CHAIN REACTION

WORDS AND MUSIC BY
JOE SAMPLE

CHICAGO SONG

BY MARCUS MILLER

Eb Version

Rise

BY RANDY BADAZZ
AND ANDY ARMER

Eb Version

Shaker Song

BY JAY BECKENSTEIN

Eb Version

Silhouette

BY KENNY G

Eb Version

TOURIST IN PARADISE

BY RUSS FREEMAN

Eb VERSION

Turn Your Love Around

WORDS AND MUSIC BY JAY GRAYDON,
STEVE LUKATHER AND BILL CHAMPLIN

Eb VERSION

You Make Me Smile

BY DAVE KOZ AND JEFF KOZ

Eb VERSION

MAPUTO

BY MARCUS MILLER

MAPUTO

BY MARCUS MILLER

BLACK FROST

BY GROVER WASHINGTON, JR.
AND BOB JAMES

CHAIN REACTION

WORDS AND MUSIC BY
JOE SAMPLE

CHICAGO SONG

BY MARCUS MILLER

♪: C VERSION

RISE

BY RANDY BADAZZ
AND ANDY ARMER

Shaker Song

BY JAY BECKENSTEIN

Silhouette

BY KENNY G

𝄢: C VERSION

TOURIST IN PARADISE

BY RUSS FREEMAN

Turn Your Love Around

WORDS AND MUSIC BY JAY GRAYDON,
STEVE LUKATHER AND BILL CHAMPLIN

You Make Me Smile

BY DAVE KOZ AND JEFF KOZ

For use with all B-flat, E-flat, Bass Clef and C instruments, the **Jazz Play-Along Series** is the ultimate learning tool for all jazz musicians. With musician-friendly lead sheets, melody cues, and other split-track choices on the included audio, these first-of-a-kind packages help you master improvisation while playing some of the greatest tunes of all time.

FOR STUDY, each tune includes a split track with: melody cue with proper style and inflection • professional rhythm tracks • choruses for soloing • removable bass part • removable piano part.

FOR PERFORMANCE, each tune also has: an additional full stereo accompaniment track (no melody) • additional choruses for soloing.

To see full descriptions of all the books in the series, visit: